I0820250

CREATIVE CAREERS

Creative Careers in FILM, TV, and THEATER

James Roland

San Diego, CA

For more information, contact:
ReferencePoint Press, Inc.
PO Box 27779
San Diego, CA 92198
www.ReferencePointPress.com

LIBRARY OF CONGRESS CATALOGING-IN-PUBLICATION DATA

Names: Roland, James, author
Title: Creative careers in film, tv, and theater / by James Roland.
Description: San Diego, CA : ReferencePoint Press, 2025. | Series: Creative careers | Includes bibliographical references and index.
Identifiers: LCCN 2025008049 (print) | LCCN 2025008050 (ebook) | ISBN 9781678210267 library binding | ISBN 9781678210274 ebook
Subjects: LCSH: Motion pictures--Vocational guidance--Juvenile literature | Television--Vocational guidance--Juvenile literature | Theater--Vocational guidance--Juvenile literature
Classification: LCC PN1995.9.P75 D68 2025 (print) | LCC PN1995.9.P75 (ebook) | DDC 791.4023--dc23/eng/20250509
LC record available at https://lccn.loc.gov/2025008049
LC ebook record available at https://lccn.loc.gov/2025008050

Contents

Introduction: Inspiring Audiences Through Creativity and Imagination

When Disney set out to bring its classic film *The Lion King* to Broadway, one of the production's many challenges was how to have actors depict the lions, hyenas, and other animals in the story. Instead of a show featuring performers in animal costumes, like the feline characters in the long-running stage musical *Cats*, the producers wanted something unique. So they turned to Julie Taymor, a veteran stage director and inventive costume designer.

Early in her career, Taymor studied two ancient types of Indonesian theater. They included topeng, a musical drama that features actors wearing colorful, highly expressive masks; and wayang, a form of puppetry in which large puppets are seen only as shadows behind a lighted screen. She put both of those influences together, along with a fascination for African and Asian art and culture, to create a breathtaking stage experience that has made *The Lion King* one of the longest-running and most popular shows in Broadway history. In his review for *Variety* after the show's 1997 Broadway debut, theater critic Greg Evans highlighted Taymor's captivating creations, including those performed in Bunraku style—a traditional Japanese form of puppetry featuring large characters with lifelike movements and expressions. Evans wrote:

> The animal creations that amble through the audience are nothing less than works of art, impressionistic and utterly graceful. Some are puppets—a wooden, Bunraku-style leopard, leaping antelope—while others are costumes—men on stilts for the giraffes, a huge elephant with a man in each leg. As often as not, the boundaries between costume, puppetry and mask are blurred, if not obliterated, in inventions that draw audible gasps from the audience.[1]

Among the most striking aspects of the costume design are the animal character masks worn above the heads of the actors. Taymor says she wanted to show animals and humans at the same time. And she deliberately wanted audiences to see the actors on stilts creating the giraffes and to see how the actors controlled the puppets. "We didn't want to hide the strings or the rods, but rather expose the mechanics and let the art of making theatre become part of the experience,"[2] she told the *Guardian* newspaper.

Taymor won Tony Awards for directing *The Lion King* and for its costume design. Besides that play, she has directed operas and movies. And though she has reached a high point in her career, her story is not that different from the countless other individuals who have channeled their creative talents and ideas into careers in theater, film, or television.

The Storytellers

Costume designers, directors, actors, writers, and all the people involved with staging a play or shooting a movie or TV show are there to tell stories—to take their audiences on a journey. In an interview with Oprah Winfrey, Taymor said, "An artist is an entertainer, number one—a storyteller who takes people someplace, who gives them what they didn't know they wanted. A performance can have amazing visuals and special effects, but it has to tell a good story, even if that story isn't original."[3]

For creative people who want to tell stories and entertain audiences, the theater, film, and television industries offer a wide array of careers to apply their skills and work with other similarly imaginative individuals.

Finding Your Way

It is not uncommon to hear stories of people who have followed a path to creative careers in film, TV, and theater starting young.

Steven Spielberg grew up a movie fan, and at age twelve he borrowed his father's 8 mm home movie camera to make his own short films with his friends. Los Angeles stage actor Isaiah Anthony needed one more class to fill out his eleventh-grade schedule in high school, so he took a theater course—and it set him on a path to the professional stage. "My advice to everyone who's thinking about pursuing acting is to believe in yourself, have confidence, and take classes,"[4] Anthony told the online magazine VoyageATL.

Signing up for school drama programs, enrolling in community theater, and shooting and editing videos are just some of the ways young people can take their first steps toward careers in theater, film, and television. From there, college programs, internships, and apprenticeships offer other opportunities to build necessary skills. These talents are in demand not just in Hollywood or on Broadway but everywhere creative people want to get together to tell stories and make audiences laugh, cry, feel, and think about themselves and their world in new ways.

Actor

Anne Hathaway has played a lot of different roles. She has been a princess, a jewel thief, and a spy. She has also lent her voice to animated films. As much as she has enjoyed a successful career filled with dramatic and comedic roles, Hathaway told *Variety* magazine in 2023 that one of the best parts about her job is hearing from fans about how they return to those films frequently when they need some escape from the real world. She said: "It is such a sweet feeling to know that you're kind of woven into someone's life. I can't describe the honor of knowing that I'm involved in the moments where people need comfort. It makes me really excited that my journey as a performer has connected with people. I love [when] projects have a life beyond their initial release."[5]

Connecting with the audience is at the heart of an actor's job, regardless of whether it is in film, television, or theater. While a very small percentage of actors have a career like Hathaway's, they all seek to play characters that will add depth to a story. Some play heroes and some villains, but regardless of the role, actors hope to evoke an emotional response—good or bad—from audiences.

At a Glance

Number of Jobs
About 76,700

Pay
$20.50 an hour, but the rate can climb considerably

Educational Requirements
None, but many have at least some college

Personal Qualities
Creativity, perseverance, confidence

Working Conditions
Long hours, often including nights and weekends

Future Job Outlook
Growth of about 5 percent through 2033

What Does an Actor Do?

Actors might perform on a theatrical stage or on film in a movie or TV show. Their job is to embody the emotions, thoughts, challenges, and triumphs of the characters they are playing. They try to lose themselves in their characters so that audiences connect with the individuals they portray.

Actors are also storytellers, and that is what draws many of them to the profession. That was especially true for Paul Rudd (Ant-Man in the Marvel franchise movies), who realized his passion was acting when he attended the University of Kansas. He said in Acting Magazine, "I was actually studying history at college, but I felt this incredible pull to acting. I loved telling stories, making people laugh. When I switched to drama, I just felt at home. It was like everything clicked."[6]

To get a part in a show, most actors must audition. They spend much of their time preparing for and going to auditions. When actors have been cast in a production, they devote their time to studying their characters, learning their lines, and rehearsing their scenes with other actors. Then it is time to perform either onstage or before a camera, bringing the story and character to life.

How Do You Become an Actor?

Most actors take acting classes in school or at actors' studios. When the opportunity to audition for a coveted part arises, they test their skills, sometimes alongside dozens or hundreds of other actors trying to get hired.

Many actors also hire agents, who help them get auditions and guide their careers. To get an agent, actors must get professional headshots—high-quality photographs that capture their looks and their personality—and have a current résumé listing their acting training and experience. Sometimes agents send these to directors looking to hire actors for new movies, TV shows, or stage

Get Ready to Audition . . . a Lot

"Auditioning IS the job of an actor! Most actors think the booking or the set work is the job and while that's part of it, auditioning is the main event. Think about it, how often do you audition compared to how often you work? Keep in mind that this is a numbers game. I'm betting you audition 80% of the time and work 20%. True, some actors may have higher booking ratios, but more often than not, most have a 10 to 1 ratio. It is just the reality of industry. . . . As you do more and more, [auditions] will become a little easier!"

—April Hartman, actor and acting coach

April Hartman, "Everything You Need to Know About Acting Auditions," TBell Actors Studio, January 12, 2021. https://tbellactorsstudio.com.

plays. An actor usually carries this portfolio to casting directors during auditions as well. And whenever possible, actors put together "demo reels," which are video compilations of their acting. These might be clips from actual plays, movies, or other professional or amateur projects they have done, as well as scenes from their acting classes or even scenes they shot at their homes or on location somewhere.

Education and Training

Many successful actors never went to college, or they enrolled but never graduated. However, many working actors today have theater degrees and years of experience acting in their college drama programs. Denise Simon, a New York City–based acting coach, told *Backstage* magazine, "A college theater program will give you the training and skills needed to excel as an actor. The right college theater program for you will give you a well-rounded education in speech movement, acting technique, stagecraft, theater history and even learning how to navigate the business of show business."[7]

Director Robert Zemeckis and actor Anne Hathaway appear on the set of the 2020 film *The Witches*. Actors like Hathaway embody the emotions, thoughts, challenges, and triumphs of the characters they play.

Many actors, including those with established careers, continue to work with acting coaches to hone their craft. Actors often study stage combat (fighting techniques), foreign languages to help master accents, singing, dancing, and other skills. Many comedic actors hone their skills by joining improvisational comedy troupes, such as the Groundlings in Los Angeles or the Upright Citizens Brigade in Chicago.

Internships

Acting internships tend to be more common in the theater, rather than in film or television. Summer high school and college internships in small and large theater companies are common and often allow students to get some acting experience, as well as learn other backstage skills, such as carpentry, lighting, and other tasks. Many theaters around the country offer year-round internships to students or recent graduates.

Skills and Personality

Actors are creative and good communicators. Actors also need to have a lot of perseverance and resilience, since they can face a lot of rejection and criticism. For most actors, it can take years of training and auditioning and working at their craft before they find success. And according to legendary actress Meryl Streep, one of the most important traits an actor needs is curiosity. She explains, "All people contain mystery, and when you act, you want to plumb that mystery until everything is known to you. . . . I'm curious about people. That's the essence of my acting. I'm interested in what it would be like to be you."[8]

On the Job

Actors fortunate enough to get hired for a Broadway show or the national tour of a play may work consistently for months at a time. Landing a recurring role in a television series can also result in months or years of steady work. But for many actors, a job can last as little as one day shooting a commercial or being an extra in a single scene in a film or TV show. Most jobs are somewhere in between.

Employers

In the theater, producers hire actors to perform in their productions. Some theaters also employ a group of actors, referred to as a repertory company, and those actors make up the casts of whatever plays the theater puts on in a season.

Film and television actors usually work for a production company that has cast them in a film or series. Companies making TV and radio commercials also hire actors. Many actors also work for theme parks and cruise lines (for onboard shows), and at other venues, for things like corporate functions and even elaborate marriage proposals or birthday parties. Voice actors are also prevalent today because of the growth of both the animation and video game industries.

Actors Must Be Adaptable

"I think that adaptability is the strongest suit you can have as an actor. . . . As an actor, particularly if you're not the leader of the project, you try to make yourself as clay-like, as malleable as possible—a blip in the radar, a wallflower, somebody who comes prepared and is ready to go and maybe have an idea or trick up your sleeve, something you want to try out. But ultimately, your responsibility is to the character for the story, to that sequence of that day, and just trying to do the best as possible."

—Timothée Chalamet, actor

Quoted in Casting Frontier, "Timothée Chalamet on the Craft of Acting," February 8, 2021. https://castingfrontier.com.

Working Conditions

Television shows and movies are shot in studios or on location. That could mean a lush, tropical island or an abandoned warehouse in the middle of a cold winter. In any case, movie and TV work can mean long hours, often at night and on weekends. And for the actors, much of that time may be spent waiting around until the lights, microphones, cameras, and other equipment are ready to go. "There's a lot of waiting around on a film set. The saying is 'hurry up and wait.' I had to learn to conserve energy when I could,"[9] recalls actor Marchánt Davis of his first experience on a film set.

Theater work can also entail long hours and a lot of waiting around—especially if an actor has a supporting role with only a few scenes. Except for those performing in an outdoor theater or, for example, parading through Disney World as a costumed character, the working conditions for actors are usually confined to an indoor theater or rehearsal space.

Earnings and Advancement

Though a handful of actors make millions of dollars every year, most make modest salaries and often must work a second job in between acting gigs. This is true for stage actors as well as those working in television or films.

According to the Bureau of Labor Statistics (BLS), the average pay for actors is $20.50 per hour. Actors who join the Screen Actors Guild–American Federation of Television and Radio Artists make more when working on films, television series, or plays whose production companies pay union rates. For example, actors in a film with a budget of more than $2 million will make at least $1,204 per day at union scale. Those with larger roles will be paid even more.

As actors gain more experience, they can often land larger roles in bigger projects. This can lead to better paychecks. Also, some actors advance by becoming directors or by producing their own projects. Reese Witherspoon, for example, is an in-demand actor in film and television. But she also runs a production company that produces movies and TV shows. If she appears in those productions, she essentially gets paid twice—as an actor and producer.

What Is the Future Outlook for Actors?

As long as audiences crave entertainment, there will always be a need for actors. And today roles are diverse, and the opportunities for actors of different ethnicities and appearances are growing, thus increasing the number of roles available. Partly because of this, acting jobs are estimated to grow by about 5 percent through 2033, according to the BLS.

Find Out More

Backstage

www.backstage.com

This website lists acting jobs around the world, from extras in big-budget movies to parts in small theater and film projects, as well as voice-over and commercial jobs. Visitors can also read articles from *Backstage* magazine, with advice on auditioning and countless other acting topics.

Playbill

https://playbill.com

Playbill is best known for publishing the programs patrons receive when they attend a play. However, the Playbill site is packed with news about the theater; interviews with scenic designers, directors, and other stage professionals; job listings; and links to shows on Broadway and elsewhere.

StageMilk

www.stagemilk.com

StageMilk is a go-to site for everything from free downloadable monologues for teens to tips for how to learn lines, information on how to get into a good drama school, and other aspects of acting. There are also lists of all-time great plays as well as articles filled with acting tips and career advice.

Scriptwriter

The wild, multiverse saga of *Everything Everywhere All at Once* tells the story of Evelyn, who owns a laundromat with her husband. Evelyn faces multiple difficulties that impact her business and her relationships with her husband and her daughter. What seem like topics for a standard drama become something else when Evelyn is told that there are parallel universes that reflect choices in life, and she is bounced through time and across dimensions to battle a version of her daughter who is bent on destroying all realities. Written by Daniel Kwan and Daniel Scheinert, who both won Academy Awards for the movie's screenplay, the film breaks a lot of screenplay "rules" of standard structure and storytelling.

At a Glance

Number of Jobs
About 5,000 writers for TV and film, far fewer for the stage

Pay
$73,000

Educational Requirements
None, but many have at least some college

Personal Qualities
Passion for storytelling, creativity, persistence, flexibility

Working Conditions
Often self-employed, may work long hours on deadline

Future Job Outlook
Growth of about 5 percent through 2033

But that was by design, says Kwan, who set out with Scheinert to make a movie like no one had seen before. Kwan said in an interview on the website Screen Daily:

> When we were in film school, someone told me, "If you want to be successful, you either have to be the best or the first." I knew as a 19-year-old I'll never

> be the best. So I'm going to see if I can be the first. A story might entertain us, it might make us think, but it won't fully affect us unless it's something completely new. Something that takes you off guard. Something that can bypass the intellect. I realized there was power in our ability to create something new.[10]

What Does a Scriptwriter Do?

The people who write scripts for movies and television are called screenwriters, while those who write for the stage are called playwrights. Though the titles are different, the jobs are the same.

When writers have an idea (whether it is their own or one they are hired to develop), they usually start the script writing process by coming up with an outline. Usually, the outline is divided into short sections called scenes. The writer then uses the outline to compose the first draft of the script. Writing a full-length screenplay or stage play can take months or years. During that time, a writer may rewrite some scenes dozens of times, eliminate others, and draft new ones.

The rewriting and polishing part of the job is crucial to success, says Richard Walter, chair of the graduate program in screenwriting at the University of California, Los Angeles. He says it is important not to rush out and try to sell a script that still needs work. "If you give yourself the time, in terms of getting the script ready and getting the career ready, you will succeed,"[11] he posted on the screenwriting site Writers Store.

Lucky scriptwriters draft scripts on assignment from a production company, but many writers create works on speculation, or on spec, that must be shopped around. If a writer with a completed spec script has an agent, the agent will send the script to producers or studios looking for new material. Writers without agents use their spec scripts to get an agent who will

Engaging Audiences Page by Page

"A good script has to be compelling, it has to make me lean forward. It has to make me wonder what is going to happen to this character; are they going to achieve their goal? Are they going to learn something? Every page, every scene, should make you want to go on this journey with this character."

—Barry Blaustein, screenwriter and writing professor

Quoted in Jeff Heimbuch, "Screenwriting: Where the Story Begins," Chapman University, March 9, 2017. https://blogs.chapman.edu.

represent them. Some beginning screenwriters and playwrights submit scripts to writing contests, hoping they can earn awards and recognition that will help them land an agent or at least get someone to read their scripts. Playwright Christina Ham used this approach early in her career. She told the Playwrights' Center, "As a playwright you will have to do your research and understand that not all contests and awards are created equally in order to gain the necessary access that you are looking for with some of the larger theaters. But, with smaller theaters, these smaller accolades may be just enough to provide an introduction and get your work in the door."[12]

Depending on the nature of the script, writers may spend a lot of time doing research. This could include studying a particular historical era, interviewing or shadowing someone in a particular field, or learning about a particular place where the story takes place.

How Do You Become a Scriptwriter?

Anyone who wants to work as a scriptwriter should start by writing and editing a narrative. Taking courses can help, and studying scripts written by others can also be useful. Some scriptwriters write alone; others work with other writers. All generally use editors or edit their own work to make sure it meets the expectations of the market and the producers who might back the project.

Education and Training

Many college film programs include a concentration in screenwriting. The same is true for theater programs that allow students to focus on playwriting. Aspiring scriptwriters can also take online courses and study with established writers who teach on the side. Some film and television production companies provide screenwriting fellowships, which are like extended workshops for up-and-coming writers. There are also some nonprofit arts foundations that award fellowships to promising playwrights.

Skills and Personality

The main skill required for success as a scriptwriter is a gift for writing and storytelling. Scriptwriters must also be able to handle rejection and criticism—both constructive and not-so-constructive. Playwright Emma Carter told radio station KCUR 89.3, "You can't just sit at home and write your play and expect to just go out and do it. You have to talk with people and share it with people and get critiques from people you trust and respect."[13]

And because it can take a long time (if ever) to find success, scriptwriters must also be determined to keep writing and keep trying. Once they finish one script, writers move on to the next.

On the Job

When scriptwriters are not at the keyboard knocking out scene after scene, they are often brainstorming ideas, pitching new ideas to producers, or talking with directors or others involved with the production of their script. To help with their own projects, scriptwriters read other scripts to learn what makes them work, and then they return to crafting their own projects. As screenwriter Scott Myers wrote in an article on Medium, "When you're a writer, you're basically never not working."[14]

Employers

Before buying a script, movie studios or production companies typically option it, usually paying the writer a small percentage of the purchase price (if there is eventually a sale). Optioning a script means a producer holds the rights to a script for a specific period to see if they can get a director and other people interested in turning that script into a film, television series, or play. If nothing happens during the option period, the rights revert to the writer, who can shop it out again.

Television writers are usually hired by a production company or network to write multiple episodes for a series. In some cases, a writer (or writers) will be hired to write a single episode, but typically a series employs a regular team of writers.

Working Conditions

Writing is often a solitary business. Scriptwriters write on their own schedule, unless they have a deadline. In those cases they may have to put in long hours to deliver the script on time. Unless they have a writing partner, completing a script is often done alone. They may work in person or remotely with a director who is producing their script or with a producer who has optioned a story.

On a film, a writer may be brought to the set to help with rewrites. But generally, once filming has started, the screenwriter's job is done. On a television series, a staff of writers is responsible for each episode. They usually work in offices located on the lot where the series is shot. They may also do rewrites during shooting, but often TV writers are busy working on scripts for future episodes.

In the theater, a playwright is often present during rehearsals, ready to make changes that the director suggests. Playwrights

Write a Play, Then Produce It

"There is a lot to be said for making a real commitment to your work and producing it yourself. This doesn't need to be a Broadway production. If you can assemble a good team of theater artists, you can mount a streamlined production of your play in a small venue without spending a ton of money."

—Will Dunne, playwright and writing teacher

Quoted in Carol Saller, "You Wrote a Play, but Now What? Advice from Dramatist Will Dunne," *Writer, Editor, Helper* (blog), Subversive Copy Editor. www.subversivecopyeditor.com.

may also be present for rewrites when a play is in previews. That is when a show is performed before a live audience in a small theater before it moves on to a bigger venue. Audience reactions can help writers, directors, and actors know what parts of the play are working well and what sections may need revision.

Earnings and Advancement

The Writers Guild of America, the organization that represents writers in television and film, reports that only about five thousand writers make a living from screenwriting. The average salary is about $73,000, though many writers make much less, while the most successful scriptwriters can make millions of dollars for their work.

As with most jobs in the arts, scriptwriters tend to advance in their careers by having success at the lower levels and working their way up to bigger projects. A playwright with works produced by regional theaters may eventually find success on Broadway. A screenwriter who has success with a low-budget film may get tapped to write a script for a bigger project. And a staff TV writer may eventually get to write and produce a series.

What Is the Future Outlook for Scriptwriters?

A relatively small number of people work full time as scriptwriters. But there is always a demand for new voices in film, television, and theater. The Bureau of Labor Statistics projects that the demand for script writing will grow by about 5 percent through 2033. For people who love to write and are willing to work at improving their skills and getting their scripts to those who can help get them produced, being a scriptwriter can be a rewarding career.

Find Out More

American Theatre Wing

https://americantheatrewing.org

The American Theatre Wing is best known for sponsoring Broadway's Tony Awards, but its main purpose is promoting theater education. This site is packed with theater resources, including a Master Class series of videos featuring playwrights, directors, and other theater professionals.

Film Courage

https://filmcourage.com

This site features fascinating articles, interviews, and videos about all aspects of filmmaking, with a special focus on screenwriting. Visitors can learn how writers improve their craft and how they navigate the business side of writing for film and television.

Internet Movie Database (IMDb)

www.imdb.com

IMDb is a go-to site for information about film and television around the world. Looking up writers and other artists will display all their credits. The site also contains video interviews, links to interesting articles, and lists of must-see movies.

Director

Jon Favreau has directed beloved movies, such as *Elf* and *Iron Man*. They are filled with memorable visuals, like Santa Claus's sleigh gliding over Central Park and Tony Stark donning his flying suit to battle villains. But Favreau, who started out in show business as an actor and writer, says the big splashy scenes are not what he wants most out of his movies.

At a Glance

Number of Jobs
About 167,900 (including producers)

Pay
$85,000, but the rate can climb considerably

Educational Requirements
None, but many have at least some college

Personal Qualities
Creative, organized, able to multitask

Working Conditions
Long hours, often including nights and weekends

Future Job Outlook
Growth of 8 percent through 2033

In an interview with the newsletter of the Directors Guild of America, *DGA Quarterly*, Favreau says he is usually much more focused on the characters and their emotional journey: "I don't come from the visual filmmaking side of movies. I come from the writing-acting-storytelling side. Rarely do I have—maybe two or three in a whole movie—a visual image that I want to chase. It usually is an emotion I want to chase, or a feeling or a character progression that I understand. That's what leads the way for me."[15]

What Does a Director Do?

Directors oversee all the creative parts of a production. They are involved in casting the main actors, revising the script, and approving costumes, set designs, visual effects, and—for films and television shows—locations for shooting. Once a production is cast, directors also work with the actors so that their performances line up with the guiding vision for the story. Directors tell actors where to go or stand and give them advice on how to deliver their lines. In film and television, directors also make decisions about camera angles, lighting, sound, editing, and camera shots that may not include any actors, such as the exterior of a building in which the action takes place.

Jon M. Chu, who directed *Crazy Rich Asians* and *Wicked*, likens the job of a director to his father cooking at the family restaurant when Chu was a child. It is hard work and not always glamorous, but it can be so rewarding. His dad split his time at the restaurant. He was sometimes out front, calmly greeting diners and making them feel relaxed and welcome. Moments later, Chu says, his father would be "greasy in the back of the kitchen, sweating. The guy that in the back of the kitchen, that was my hero. Not the guy who's making the jokes, but the guy in the back working his butt off. . . . I think about that often in my own life: I want to be the guy in the kitchen."[16]

How Do You Become a Director?

Directors often work in other aspects of film, television, and theater before getting the chance to call all the shots. Christopher McQuarrie, who has directed several *Mission: Impossible* films, started out as a screenwriter. Greta Gerwig, who directed *Barbie*, started out as an actress, appearing in numerous movies before launching her directing career. Other film directors work as cinematographers (for film or television), assistant directors (for stage or screen), producers, or in other aspects of their field until they get a chance to direct.

Usually, a person's first chance to direct is for a smaller, low-budget production. This is because producers usually do not want to take a chance with an unproven director in charge of an expensive, major production. Steven Spielberg, for example, who makes films with budgets over $100 million, started out directing TV shows in his twenties before he was hired to direct movies.

Theater directors also tend to begin their careers doing other related jobs, such as actor, choreographer, or stage manager. And they also often get their first directing opportunities in community theater or other smaller productions.

Education and Training

Directors working in film and television often major in subjects such as cinema arts (film) in college, making student films before trying to break into the movie or television business. Likewise, theatrical directors usually study drama in college and direct student productions whenever possible. This gives these aspiring directors the practical experience and technical expertise they will need in their professional careers.

Internships

Future directors can sometimes jump-start their careers through internships with various production companies, theaters, or organizations, such as the American Film Institute or the Apollo Theater. Because being a director involves so many aspects of a production, internships for aspiring directors typically expose students to many different jobs. In addition to learning about directing, theater interns may learn about stage management and technical theater (lights and sound), while film or television interns may learn about editing, cinematography, and other roles in a production.

Certification and Licensing

Directors do not need a certification or license to work in film or theater. However, most directors working in movies or television are members of the Directors Guild of America. Similarly, the Stage Directors and Choreographers Society represents most professional stage directors and choreographers.

Believe You Can Do It

"Start believing in yourself. Because if you don't think there's a place for you in the industry there won't be. I had to decide I wanted to direct. No one was ever going to tell me I should direct or make that happen. You have to decide for yourself what you want and trust who you are."

—Makenna Fojas, University of Washington student filmmaker

Quoted in Nancy Joseph, "Making Films, Finding Community," University of Washington College of Arts & Sciences, May 31, 2023. https://artsci.washington.edu.

Skills and Personality

Directors are creative people who must also be highly organized. They have to be decisive and willing to delegate responsibilities to other members of the production team. To be successful, directors need to be able to include others in their creative process. "I get to take things that were previously in one dimension and put them into three dimensions using my imagination and intellect and people skills,"[17] Broadway director Kimberly Senior told *Backstage*.

On the Job

Film and television directors are on the job with every project long before the cast is assembled and the cameras start rolling. The planning and preparation require countless decisions and hours spent working with other members of the production team. And after shooting is over, directors are still at work, overseeing the editing, scoring (adding music to the finished product), and other tasks.

For theater directors, there is less technical work to oversee, and once their shows open, they are less involved in the day-to-day run of a play. Sometimes they may make changes in blocking

Guided by a director, dancers perform a scene for an upcoming production. Directors oversee the creative parts of a production. This can include casting, script revisions, costumes, set designs, and visual effects.

(the positioning and movement of the actors onstage) or other parts of a show when it is in previews or during the early part of a show's run.

Employers

Movie production companies, such as A24 and Happy Madison Productions, or studios, such as Paramount Pictures and the Walt Disney Company, select directors to helm individual projects. In television, directors are hired by production companies, networks, or streaming services. A TV series may have one director for all episodes, multiple directors for different episodes, or a new director for each one. This can also provide an opportunity for actors in these shows to step into a directing role.

In theater, producers (the people putting up the money for the play) hire a director. Theater companies, such as the Guthrie Theater in Minneapolis and the Signature Theatre Company in New

York City, hire freelance directors for specific shows or use staff directors, who are employees of the company and direct plays year after year for those organizations.

Working Conditions

Directors, like other members of a production team, work long hours. The work of a theater director is usually confined to a stage and rehearsal studio, while a film or television director may work in a studio, also known as a soundstage, or on location, such as a real city street, beach, desert, or private home.

In postproduction, film directors work closely with editors to take raw footage and cut it down to a version that matches the director's vision. This process can take weeks or months, but it is essential for the final product to be what the director wants. Television series directors must work at a faster pace, with less time available in pre- and postproduction. Their shooting schedules are also tighter than those of most movies, with little time or budget for scenes taking place far from the studios, where most TV series are shot.

Earnings and Advancement

The average income for stage or screen directors is about $85,000. Some may make much less, while those at the top end can earn millions per project. Independent filmmakers who must raise money to finance their projects typically do not make a lot, unless a studio buys their film and agrees to distribute it. Theatrical directors working in community theater often make less than the average, but those working on Broadway, for example, usually earn six-figure incomes.

Directors commonly start with smaller productions and gradually work their way up to bigger, more expensive projects. Directors who are talented, dedicated, and can work well with others will have the best opportunities for career advancement.

Work with Those Who Inspire You

"You must gravitate to the most talented people you know and find some way to get close to them—to work with them, to observe them, to be around them. That's the finishing school of directing: when you get around people you admire, whose aesthetic matches your own."

—Jack O'Brien, Tony Award–winning Broadway director

Quoted in Casey Mink, "How to Become a Theater Director," *Backstage*, April 12, 2021. www.backstage.com.

What Is the Future Outlook for Directors?

Opportunities for stage and screen directors should continue to grow in the years ahead, with some forecasts projecting 8 percent growth through 2033. Streaming services, such as Netflix and Apple TV+, have created outlets for movies and TV shows that might not have been made by the traditional film studios and television networks. Long-time director Paul Feig says that since the major studios are more selective about the films they finance, filmmakers will find more opportunities with the streaming services. "We'd all love to be making theatrical films with big releases but with the studios cutting back on their output, the streamers have really stepped up to let us tell our stories with real budgets,"[18] he said in an interview with Dark Horizons.

Find Out More

American Film Institute (AFI)

www.afi.com

This site presents the history of film and opportunities to join the next generation of filmmakers. It assembles lists of must-see great films in a variety of genres and allows visitors to watch short movies made by filmmakers who studied at the AFI. The organization operates a film school in Los Angeles and offers online classes to interested film students.

Careers in Film

www.careersinfilm.com

This site presents information on a variety of film careers, including directing. There are "Industry Insights" articles about internships, tips to start a filmmaking career, and more. It also provides an up-to-date list of top film schools in the United States and around the world.

Dramatics

https://dramatics.org

Dramatics is the official student website of the International Thespian Society. It houses articles about directing, acting, and other jobs in the theater. It also details college theater programs and offers advice about how to get a jump-start on a theater career.

Production Designer

Bringing the Emerald City to life in the stage version of *Wicked* required a set built with shiny, reflective materials, giant cutout windows to give the "city" a sense of depth and grandeur, and of course, plenty of green lighting. For the film version of the award-winning musical, the Emerald City sets were even grander, featuring green glass bricks, lush curtains, glistening fountains, structures more than 40 feet (12.2 m) tall, and countless other elements to create the look of a real city.

The final version of the movie's Emerald City was also enhanced by computer-generated imagery (CGI) after filming was completed. For production designer Nathan Crowley, though, it was important to have solid sets through which the actors could move, rather than create most of the Emerald City on a computer. "The joy is that it all feels very real," Crowley told *Architectural Digest* in 2024. "CGI can distance the audience, but architecture really holds you."[19]

In many ways the job of a production designer is to create a world for the actors to inhabit that also welcomes the audience into the story.

At a Glance

Number of Jobs
About 29,600

Pay
$59,490

Educational Requirements
Degree not required, but training in studio or visual arts, theater, or film is beneficial

Personal Qualities
Imagination, artistic vision, ability to work well with others

Working Conditions
In an art studio and on a set, typically requiring evening and weekend time commitments

Future Job Outlook
Growth of 5 percent through 2033

What Does a Production Designer Do?

Every story, whether on-screen or onstage, requires locations. The action might take place aboard starships and on wild, alien planets like in the *Guardians of the Galaxy* movies or in a simple attic apartment like in the play *The Diary of Anne Frank*. The people responsible for creating those distinct environments—from the sets and props to the lighting, camera angles, and graphics—are called production designers. In the theater, they are also known as stage designers or scenic designers.

Production designers usually start a project by reading a script and brainstorming with the director about how scenes within the story should look. They also consider what mood, emotion, or aspects of the character they want the set to accentuate. For example, in the movie *Wonka*, Willy Wonka builds a candy shop inspired by the home and garden he shared with his mother before they were separated. Crowley explained to *Variety*, "It's a memory of his childhood that he was most happy in with his mother, and you translate that into an edible shop, as his memory of his past. The most beautiful thing he can think of is that. So he wants the secret garden of his childhood in chocolate and sweets so that they have to connect."[20]

Production design involves selecting paint colors, fabrics, props, furniture, artwork, lighting, and other design elements that serve the story. In film and television, the action may take place on a real city street or in an existing office building or home. But even those real-world locations are often altered by adding things like storefront signs, cars, personal items the characters would have around them, and other props that are appropriate to the time and place. Fantasy or science fiction stories must also contain set designs that make an audience believe in the reality of those imagined worlds.

To realize their visions, production designers supervise a production's art department, which includes an art director, painters, carpenters, prop masters, and others whose responsibility is to translate the description of a scene in the script into a three-dimensional set.

Production designers also spend a lot of time doing research and looking for inspiration. If a scene takes place during a historical period, a production designer will study photos or drawings from that era to re-create an authentic version of it.

How Do You Become a Production Designer?

There is no traditional path to becoming a production designer, though most of them have some formal art training. Production designers often start their careers by taking whatever jobs they can get in theater or film. Hannah Beachler, the production designer for *Black Panther*, started as a set dresser—the person who arranges the props, furniture, and other elements of a scene before the camera rolls—and says she worked just about every job in an art department before moving up to production designer. It is a common career path and one that can be very helpful. "Learn everything, because it will inform you when you get to production design,"[21] Beachler told *Backstage*.

Education and Training

Production designers have a strong background in visual arts or design, often studying art or architecture in college. Many also earn degrees in theater or film. David Crank, the production designer for *Knives Out* and other movies, studied studio art at the College of William & Mary and then earned a master of fine arts in theater design from Carnegie Mellon University. He took jobs with scenic art crews in theaters around the country, eventually working his way up to art director and then production designer. He told *Backstage* that you learn the job by taking whatever jobs you can to further your skills and knowledge of the industry. He explains, "Training in design, drawing, and drafting is important. It

It Is All About Collaboration and Organization

"As a production designer, I am responsible for the overall look of the project. By working with the director's vision, what the script dictates, what the cinematographer needs and requests, as well as practical locations and/or set builds I come up with how and what the final project looks like. Sometimes this is very planned out and sometimes we work on the fly and come up with solutions to problems. It is incredibly creative but also all about organization, management and problem-solving."

—Chris Crane, film production designer

Quoted in Andrew Cheek, "Production Design in Cinema: Interview with Chris Crane," Medium, March 31, 2020. https://andrewgcheek.medium.com.

makes one's job easier. That being said, people who don't draw and draft have become brilliant designers, so maybe tenacity and inquisitiveness are better skills to have. Design is a very personal thing and I think people come up with ways of conveying their ideas that work. There is no one way to do any of this."[22]

Internships

Theater internships often expose many students to backstage jobs, including set design and construction, props, lighting, and other elements of production design. Independent film companies also recruit interns to help with their art departments and set dressing. College film or theater programs may have connections for production design internships or for opportunities to work in the art departments of film, television, or stage productions.

Skills and Personality

Production designers are artists who love to collaborate. They must be able to combine their own artistic vision with ideas from writers, directors, and others involved with a production. Because production designers oversee the art department on a film, TV show, or play, they have to be comfortable giving instructions and delegating responsibility to their crews. And they must be good problem solvers who can think on their feet and make big decisions in a hurry if necessary.

On the Job

The job demands for production designers vary greatly, depending on whether they are working in film, television, or theater. In general, though, a production designer creates sketches and prototypes of various sets, assembles a crew to build or modify needed structures, and then oversees the construction, decorating, and furnishing of the sets.

Employers

The producers of a television series will typically hire one production designer to work on all the episodes. For movies, the film production company hires the production designer. The same is true in theater. A scenic designer works for the show's producers, though the director often has some influence over which scenic designer and other members of the production crew are hired.

Working Conditions

Production designers in film, television, and theater can expect to work long hours. Their schedules are also determined by deadlines. Big-budget movies and theatrical productions may allow a production designer more time to come up with ideas and supervise the construction of sets. Smaller productions usually have less lead time, forcing production designers to come up with simpler, less expensive designs. For most television series, production designers also have to work quickly and efficiently because there is little downtime between filming episodes.

Production designers usually start their work in a studio, coming up with sketch ideas and 3-D models of possible set designs.

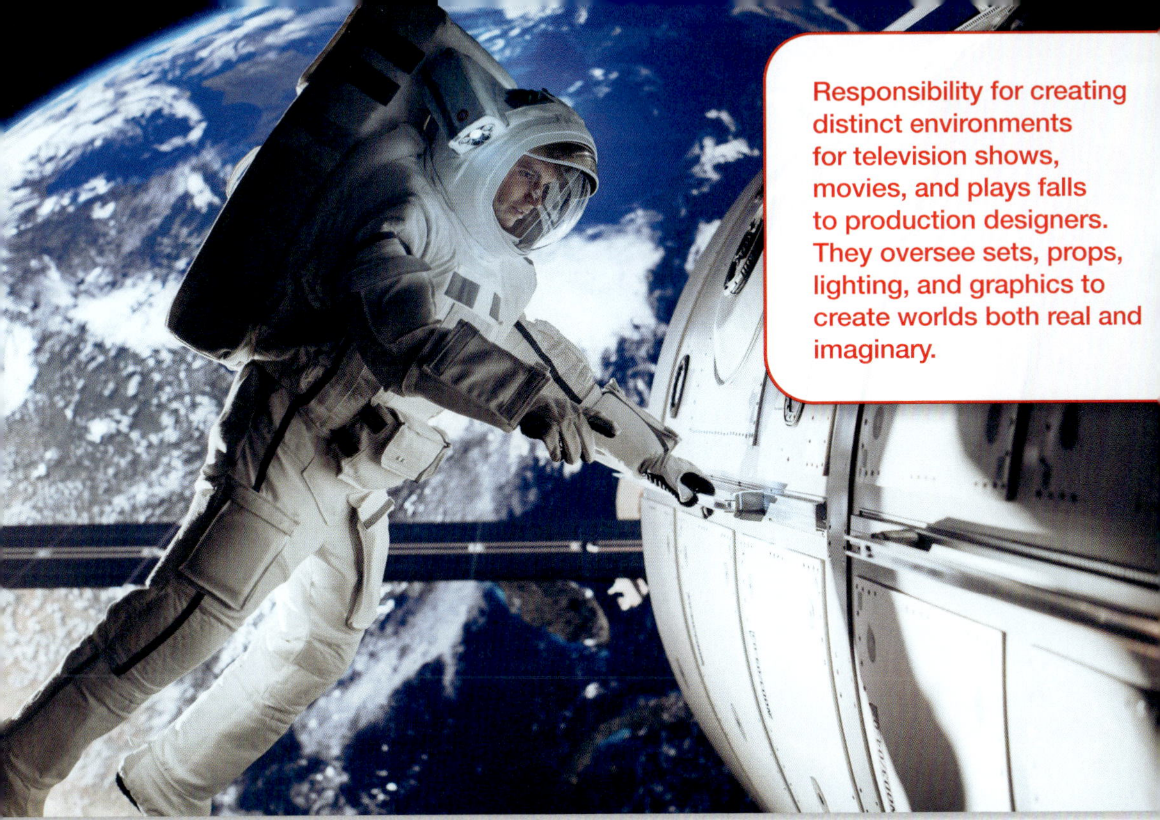

Responsibility for creating distinct environments for television shows, movies, and plays falls to production designers. They oversee sets, props, lighting, and graphics to create worlds both real and imaginary.

Then the work transfers to the set for the actual construction, painting, decorating, and other parts of creating a set. When a film or TV series plans to shoot on location—somewhere other than a studio—the production design team must scout the location and work with local officials and property owners on making any temporary changes to the look of the location.

Earnings and Advancement

Production designers are usually freelance workers who are hired to work on a specific film, play, television show, commercial, or other production. Once their work is finished on that project, they move on to the next one. A production designer working on a television series may have a long-term contract that runs for an entire season or for multiple seasons over a span of at least a few years.

As it is for everyone working on a particular play, TV show, or movie, the production's budget usually determines how much a production designer or scenic designer makes. The average

Following the Director's Lead

"When I sit down with the director to talk about a play for the first time, that conversation is a great two hour wild ride with a lot of coffee and no imagery and no ideas. I will read the play a couple of times before that meeting, but I won't form any ideas about how it should look until I talk to the director because what the director is interested in is absolutely the lead to follow. . . It's about what the director is excited about, and if the playwright is with us, what the playwright is thinking about, that's the leaping off point."

—Rachel Hauck, Tony Award–winning scenic designer

Quoted in Victoria Myers, "An Interview with Set Designer Rachel Hauck," The Interval, May 21, 2019. www.theintervalny.com.

annual income for a production designer and people in related industries is about $60,000. However, an experienced production designer working on a big-budget film could make six figures for that movie alone.

Career advancement often depends on having an agent who can help a production designer move on to bigger, more high-profile productions. Some production designers start their own businesses that include art directors and other professionals who are hired as a group to work on various projects.

What Is the Future Outlook for Production Designers?

The growth of new production design jobs is expected to be about 5 percent through 2033. As more stories are being told featuring people of color and individuals of all kinds, opportunities for a broader mix of production designers should grow, too.

Production designers are also acquiring new tools for the job. Ongoing advancements in augmented reality, for example, are allowing filmmakers to create worlds that would have been too expensive to make or even impossible to imagine just a few years ago.

Find Out More

Art Directors Guild (ADG)

https://adg.org

The ADG is the professional organization for art directors, set designers, and others who work in production design. Visitors can find information about different professions in the art departments for film and theater and more than a thousand photographs of theater, TV, and film sets to study.

Production Designers Collective

www.productiondesignerscollective.org

This site is focused solely on production design for film, theater, and television. Production designers share stories, offer advice, and discuss new developments in the industry. The site also includes links to blogs, podcasts, magazines, and other resources devoted to the craft.

Set Decorators Society of America

www.setdecorators.org

Set decoration is where many production designers start out. This site is filled with profiles of set decorators and articles about how they come up with their ideas for decorating film, television, and theater sets. The site provides a glimpse into what it is like to work on a set.

Hair and Makeup Artist

Transforming a human actor into a character that previously existed only in animated films is a team effort. It certainly takes a talented performer and costumer, but it also requires creative hair and makeup artists. For Broadway's *Shrek the Musical* team, that effort required the talents of people like Dave Presto, an award-winning makeup artist. It was his job to turn the beloved emerald ogre into a flesh-and-blood character onstage for the musical version of the classic film night after night.

Presto has also worked in film and television on much more human characters, but the creativity and effort needed to bring ogres and other fantastical creatures to life is what really makes his job fun. "Making someone look old or making them look like a character, like Popeye or something like that, even fantasy characters, those are the ones I like the most," he told Film Connection. "I like to transform someone into someone else or something else."[23]

Most hair and makeup jobs in film, theater, and television require nowhere near the amount of glue, prosthetics, and other elements

At a Glance

Number of Jobs
About 4,600

Pay
$32.97 an hour, but the rate can climb considerably

Educational Requirements
Classes and training in cosmetology

Personal Qualities
Creativity, good people skills, excellent hair and makeup skills

Working Conditions
Long hours, often including early mornings and weekends

Future Job Outlook
Growth of 6.5 percent through 2033

necessary for Shrek and his fellow imaginary creatures onstage. But all the work of the talented makeup artists and hairstylists is still an essential part of any show that seeks to turn actors into someone or something else.

What Do Hair and Makeup Artists Do?

Hair and makeup artists work with directors, producers, and actors to develop the right look for every character in a movie or show, and that might include aging or otherwise altering characters throughout the narrative if needed. There is much more to the job than applying makeup and styling a person's hair right before a performance, explains longtime Hollywood makeup artist Dick Smith. He tells *Backstage*, "There are conferences; there are sketches being made; there are discussions with the director and so forth on how he sees it. There's a lot of preparation in the sense of the designing and dealing with the makeup."[24]

If a character ages, for example, a makeup artist designs a look for each stage of aging and collaborates with a team of makeup and hair artists to apply makeup, style hair, and use wigs or prosthetics as needed to achieve the desired appearance. And if the character is an alien or a monster or other type of creature, makeup artists might become cocreators of the character by stylizing its appearance. For present-day films, TV shows, and plays, the hair and makeup jobs may be a little easier, but they are no less important.

When it is done well, the work of hair and makeup artists goes unnoticed. Audiences should be paying attention to the characters and the story, not thinking about how the actors were made to look a certain way.

How Do You Become a Hair and Makeup Artist?

There is not a clear or traditional path that most hair and makeup artists follow to work in film, television, or theater. They all have

You Have to Know Your Actors

"Some makeup artists have a really fine touch that can practically put an actor to sleep, and there are other makeup artists who may be new, and they're a little rough. You also have to kind of gauge with an actor—when it's time to go in and touch up and when it's time to leave them alone to prepare—because you can't be selfish with them. You can't consider them your piece of art. You have to give them time to prepare and not be in their face all the time, so that's something that you eventually learn with each actor."

—Mike Smithson, Hollywood makeup artist

Quoted in Cassie Carpenter, "The Magic in the Makeup," *Backstage*, November 5, 2019. www.backstage.com.

some experience and training in working with makeup or hairstyling, but otherwise they all get into their entertainment business in their own way. England's Annie Little, for example, was recruited by a friend to help with hairstyling on a television series. What she thought would be a temporary job turned into a career. She started as a trainee and now runs the hair and makeup departments for television shows and films. She tells the BBC, "You can learn a lot on the job, and every day is a learning experience, but I would say, fundamentally, you should have a basic understanding of hairdressing and makeup. . . . I think you can come to this job from different avenues: I trained as a wig maker, so that has become a very useful skill to have on set."[25]

Education and Training

Some cosmetology or makeup artistry schools, mostly in large cities, have courses or programs that feature film and theater hair and makeup. Students at Los Angeles' Cinema Makeup School, for example, learn from industry professionals. "I'm learning from some of the best in the business,"[26] movie makeup artist Ashley Hines told the *Los Angeles Times*.

Before becoming the main hair and makeup stylist for a film or play, many artists work as part of the hair and makeup team on productions. As assistants, they learn from veteran artists and gain experience on a set or backstage, an invaluable source of on-the-job training.

Volunteer Work and Internships

Aspiring hair and makeup artists can get internships through their college theater or film programs. Working professionals also need assistants, so some beginners may be able to get part-time work or even job shadowing or volunteer work as part of an apprenticeship program. Some artists get experience early on by volunteering to do hair and makeup for student-produced or independent films made in their area.

Certification and Licensing

The certification and licensing requirements for hair and makeup artists vary by state. Generally, most professionals in this field have a cosmetology license. To work in mainstream film, theater, and television productions, these specialists will need to be members of the Make-Up Artists & Hair Stylists Guild. This organization advocates for members by helping standardize pay rates and ensuring appropriate industry working conditions.

Skills and Personality

Creativity is a key trait for hair and makeup artists. They must also be good communicators, willing to take ideas from other people and incorporate them with their own designs. And because working on people's hair and makeup is such an intimate experience, it is very important to make actors feel at ease while applying makeup and prosthetics and styling their hair.

On the Job

Hair and makeup artists help plan the look of characters before a production begins, but they also work throughout the process, making adjustments and ensuring that actors maintain consistency from scene to scene—or even take to take in the case of film and television. These artists can spend long hours on sets touching up the actors' makeup and hair. Similarly, during a play, the performers' hair and makeup often require attention in between scenes.

Employers

All kinds of film, television, and theater productions need people to oversee hair and makeup. Production companies hire these artists for the duration of the production. Some stars even have their own hair and makeup people who work with them regularly.

Working Conditions

On a film and TV set, hair and makeup sessions often begin hours before shooting starts, and hair and makeup artists are on hand as long as the actors are performing in case touchups or other changes are needed. During theatrical performances, makeup artists and hairstylists do that work offstage, and they may even have to quickly alter a character's appearance if it must change from one scene to another. Most plays are presented in the evening, so the working day usually does not begin as early in the theater as it does for movies or television. Regardless of the medium, hair and makeup artists spend hours on their feet and must always be ready to step in when needed.

Another concern for hair and makeup artists—as well as the actors—is the presence of potentially harmful chemicals and minerals in the products they use. Eye makeup, for example, can contain chrome, aluminum, and other ingredients that cause al-

Hair and makeup artists work with directors, producers, and actors to develop the right look for every character. This might involve aging an actor or altering the actor's physical features in other ways, depending on the story and the demands of the role.

lergic reactions. Some artificial nail products contain formaldehyde, a toxic chemical, while the solvents used to help actors remove makeup and glued-on prosthetics can also irritate the skin. As a result, hair and makeup artists must be particularly careful handling, applying, and storing their products. Most avoid using harmful chemicals, and they often test their go-to products on small patches of an actor's skin to see whether they cause irritation.

Earnings and Advancement

Hair and makeup artists in the entertainment business make an average of about $33 an hour. Their earnings can improve significantly if they get to work on big-budget productions. Artists who have a good experience working with stars on one film or in a play may be hired again for future projects with those stars.

Collaboration Is the Key

"I have my idea of what a character should look like as I read the script, making my notes. I also know the cast is arriving with that character in them already and I need to hear how they see themselves. I take what they say, how I see it, and what the vision is of the writer or the director and try to make it a collaborative effort."

—Debi Young, Emmy-nominated makeup artist

Quoted in Ron Cassie, "Meet the Baltimore Mother and Daughter-in-Law Who 'Make Up' Hollywood," *Baltimore*, September 2024. www.baltimoremagazine.com.

What Is the Future Outlook for Hair and Makeup Artists?

Because actors want to look their best when appearing in front of an audience or a camera, there will always be a need for hair and makeup artists. Job growth of about 6.5 percent is expected through 2033. These artists help actors get into a character, whether that means accentuating the glamorous, scary, or cool sides of their performance.

The job of makeup artists is being augmented, however, by at least one recent development, the use of computer-generated imagery (CGI) to change the appearance of actors. Filmmakers are using this visual effect to make older actors look like younger versions of themselves, for example.

This technology could be viewed as a threat to the field, but Oscar-winning makeup artist Ve Neill explains that CGI can be helpful in a few ways, particularly because it can "erase" things like wrinkles, hairs out of place, or other elements that are not wanted in a shot. It can make a nose smaller, for example, which traditional makeup cannot do. "As makeup artists, we can physically only do so much and that is usually adding to the silhouette instead of removing,"[27] she says. This spirit of embracing innovation can only improve the work these professionals do to engage audiences and help bring stories to life.

Find Out More

Careers.Broadway

https://careers.broadway

The site is packed with information describing dozens of career paths in theater. Among them are makeup artists, hair and wig designers, and many others. Videos from Broadway hair and makeup artists are available, as well as links to many articles about hair and makeup art.

Cinema Makeup School, YouTube

www.youtube.com/user/cinemamakeup

The famed Hollywood makeup school's YouTube channel includes *In the Chair* interviews with leading hair and makeup artists. Other videos include presentations by current students, demonstrations of makeup techniques, and news about the hair and makeup industry.

Theatrecrafts

www.theatrecrafts.com

This British-based site covers a range of technical theater topics, including hair and makeup. There are fascinating articles and videos about the art of makeup and a helpful glossary of terms used in the craft. Visitors can also get behind-the-scenes information on dozens of stage shows.

Visual Effects Artist

When the very first *Star Wars* movie hit theaters in 1977, its groundbreaking visual effects (VFX) dazzled audiences around the world and won the team behind the light sabers and space battles an Academy Award for Best Visual Effects. But to achieve those effects, the team used, among other items, plastic models and fishing line, firecrackers, newly developed camera lenses, and large matte paintings, which are painted backdrops used in movies and television to give the illusion of city, wilderness landscape, or other settings that would be too difficult or expensive to build or film on location. Thus, many of the spectacular set pieces were created using "practical effects," or special effects not generated by computers.

When *Star Wars: The Force Awakens* was released nearly forty years after the original film, many of the starships and planets existed only on a computer. The rise of computer-generated imagery (CGI) and other VFX technology have allowed filmmakers to move beyond practical effects and stretch the bounds of what can be imagined and put on film. And even though their tools have changed, VFX artists

At a Glance

Number of Jobs
About 73,700

Pay
$47.63 an hour on average, but the rate can climb considerably

Educational Requirements
None, but many have at least some college

Personal Qualities
Imagination, advanced computer skills, enjoys collaborating

Working Conditions
Long hours, usually in studios or at home

Future Job Outlook
Growth of 4 percent through 2033

are just as inspired and excited about what they bring to a production as they were decades ago. Visual effects pioneer John Dykstra, who won an Oscar for that original *Star Wars* film, has embraced what the new technology means for his craft and that of other VFX artists in film, television, and theater. He told *American Cinematographer* magazine in 2023 that technical advances do not change how much satisfaction he gets from creating amazing visuals. He said, "I enjoy the process of interpreting the written page into ideas for images. That's something I enjoy pretty much more than anything else."[28]

What Does a Visual Effects Artist Do?

A VFX artist uses computer software to create digitally generated images that are meant to seamlessly fit into the live action of a film or television show. Scenes of Spider-Man swinging his way through New York City, the wild tornadoes in *Twisters*, the spaceships and sandworms in *Dune*, and countless other images in film and on TV are the work of VFX artists.

These artists tend to specialize in certain aspects of visual effects. Animators, for example, make computer-generated characters move. Layout artists determine a shot's framing, camera angles, and the basic lighting for a scene. And digital painters do things like cover up the wires used to make an actor appear to be flying and reconstruct computer-generated backgrounds when they become cluttered or spoiled by too much action or character movement in front of the backgrounds.

VFX artists work closely with directors and the production team to enhance storytelling by creating characters, settings, and action sequences that would be impossible or less effective without computer-generated effects.

How Do You Become a Visual Effects Artist?

VFX artists develop their skills by studying visual effects in film school and by making their own films and special effects with home digital media tools. Once students have an interesting and impressive demo reel, or portfolio, they can apply for internships and entry-level jobs at studios or with production companies.

Education and Training

Visual effects artists usually study animation, computer graphics, film, or visual arts in college. Many college film programs include a visual effects concentration. VFX professionals do not necessarily require a degree, but they do need to have a high level of technical knowledge to get started, and much of that can be learned in a classroom. Aspiring VFX artists may take courses in specific skills, such as animation or compositing, which is the art of combining separate computer-generated images, such as a background and an explosion, into one seamless shot.

Attending a school with a strong VFX program can give students a helpful preview of their future workplace. Rob Price studied animation and VFX at Full Sail University in Orlando, Florida. He said the demands of learning new skills quickly in school mirrored his experience working at Zoic Studios, which provides VFX for Netflix series and other productions. "You learn a brand new thing every month on different software, and you just need to make it work," he says of his time at Full Sail. "That's what's going to happen in the industry, too."[29]

Like a lot of his peers, Price worked entry-level jobs in VFX before getting opportunities to work on bigger projects with more responsibilities. He is now the VFX supervisor at Zoic. Many VFX artists start out as assistants, also known as runners, at studios. Their jobs might include office-type duties, such as answering phones, as well as simple VFX duties that free up time for the veteran artists to work on more complex jobs.

Internships

VFX studios, as well as major television and film studios such as Pixar and Netflix, offer internships to college students and re-

Art and Grit Go Together

"You can spend all day working on something, realize you hate it, and find yourself having to start from scratch the next day. Not a lot of people can handle that type of struggle. That's why my number one bit of advice to aspiring artists is KEEP GOING. No matter how impossible it seems, if you truly love it, Don't you dare quit. A little GRIT can go a long way."

—Matthew Munn, computer animator

Quoted in CanvasRebel, "Meet Matthew Munn," April 17, 2023. https://canvasrebel.com.

cent graduates. Organizations, including the Academy of Motion Picture Arts and Sciences, also offer prestigious summer internships. Internships can be great ways not only to learn current VFX software and tools but also to help compile a portfolio and perhaps make professional contacts that will lead to a full-time job.

Skills and Personality

Visual effects artists must be highly creative and very skilled at using digital effects technology. It is not enough to have a good imagination, possess artistic talents, and be comfortable working with a variety of software programs. Kevin Geiger, a longtime Disney VFX artist, says it is also important to be curious about how visual effects were done years ago and to be thoughtful about how the technology is going to change in the future. He told students at his alma mater, the Cleveland Institute of Art, "Be open to new ideas, new tools, new ways of working, and new reasons for working. Study what came before you, be aware of what's around you, have a vision for where you want to go and pivot as you like."[30]

VFX artists must also enjoy collaborating and be willing to take suggestions and criticism from other members of the visual effects team and the director, who is ultimately in charge of a film or show's creative elements. VFX artists also need to demonstrate the ability to think fast and respond well to the challenges that inevitably occur on every project. "Problem solving is probably the most important thing for any part of visual effects work, in my opinion,"[31] says Price.

On the Job

Working as a VFX artist means combining a love for visual storytelling with a talent and interest in the digital arts. The job can often require long hours, and the time spent often comes without the recognition that goes to actors, writers, and directors. But for those who love creating characters, settings, and action that will dazzle audiences, a VFX career may be the right choice.

Employers

VFX artists usually work for studios that exclusively provide visual effects for film and television productions, such as Industrial Light & Magic, or work for major film and TV studios that have their own VFX departments. Some VFX artists also work independently and are hired by a studio or production company for specific projects.

Working Conditions

VFX artists usually work as part of an effects team. The team may include just a few people if the effects are simple and the budget is low. A TV commercial for a laundry detergent, for example, may require a few seconds of sparkles around the clothes to show how clean they are. That is an effect one or two people can do. But in a big-budget science-fiction or action film with a lot of CGI and other visual effects, the team might include hundreds of artists, with smaller groups focused on specific aspects of the visual environment.

VFX artists typically maintain a regular work schedule, but as deadlines approach they may need to add some evenings and

The Importance of Learning by Doing

"As a kid I grew up watching *Star Wars*, the behind the scenes footage and how they produced the old school special effects. I had always been a fan of Sci-Fi and the idea of being able to create the unknown, something not real and make it look realistic, was really exciting. I started out thinking, how is this stuff even made, so it was curiosity really that led me down this path. I enjoyed art and discovered more 3D and visual effects software and started teaching myself. With any art you need to push yourself in your own time, you can't just rely on schooling."

—Charles Dockerill, visual effects artist

Quoted in My First Job in Film, "Charles Dockerill," 2021. https://myfirstjobinfilm.com.

weekends. If employed by an effects company or production studio, VFX artists are usually on-site in offices during the workday. Freelance VFX artists often work out of home studios and on their own schedule.

Earnings and Advancement

VFX artists and animators earn an average of about $47 an hour. It is worth noting that VFX artists hired to work on a production are usually paid a set amount for the project—regardless of how many hours they work. That means if additional work is needed or they have to work longer hours to meet a deadline, they do not always receive additional income.

What Is the Future Outlook for Visual Effects Artists?

The need for talented VFX artists in film and television, as well as in the gaming industry, is expected to grow by roughly 4 percent through 2033. Much of that growth will be driven by streaming services, such as Netflix and Disney+, that continue to make big-budget films and television series—many of which have science-fiction or fantasy elements. Tom Williams, managing director of DNEG Episodic, a company that provides VFX and other creative technologies for film and television, says, "Streaming has increased the demand for VFX work and accelerated the growth of all parts of the production and post-production industries."[32] The next wave of VFX artists will surely capitalize on that growth.

Find Out More

Code.org

https://code.org

The ability to code on a computer is an important skill for anyone working in visual effects. This site offers free lessons for learners of all skill levels. Visitors can learn the basics of coding and create their own animated characters, stories, and games.

Pixar in a Box

www.khanacademy.org/computing/pixar

Pixar's educational series on Khan Academy explores animation techniques used by Pixar Studios, including character animation, storytelling, and much more. The lessons are taught by Pixar animators and are open to anyone.

Visual Effects Society

www.vesglobal.org

This site hosts interviews with VFX artists in film, television, gaming, and other industries as well as in-person and online events for members and nonmembers alike. It also posts videos about various aspects of visual effects work and links to internships and other educational resources.

Source Notes

Introduction: Inspiring Audiences Through Creativity and Imagination

1. Greg Evans, "*The Lion King* (New Amsterdam Theater)," *Variety*, November 13, 1997. https://variety.com.
2. Quoted in Chris Wiegand, "Julie Taymor: How We Made The Lion King Musical," *The Guardian*, October 22, 2019. www.theguardian.com.
3. Quoted in Oprah Winfrey, "Oprah Talks to Julie Taymor," *O, the Oprah Magazine*, November 2001. www.oprah.com.
4. Quoted in VoyageATL, "Meet Isaiah Anthony," May 2, 2024. https://voyageatl.com.

Actor

5. Quoted in Zack Sharf, "Anne Hathaway: 'I Was Warned That My Career Would Fall off a Cliff at the Age of 35,' Which 'a Lot of Women Face,'" *Variety*, November 13, 2023. https://variety.com.
6. Quoted in Acting Magazine, "How Paul Rudd Got into Acting." https://actingmagazine.com.
7. Quoted in Rebecca Strassberg, "14 Industry Experts on Whether Actors Need College Degrees," *Backstage*, January 8, 2024. www.backstage.com.
8. Quoted in Vincent Andriano, "Meryl Streep Acting Advice," StageMilk, September 9, 2020. www.stagemilk.com.
9. Quoted in Boston Conservatory at Berklee, "Marchánt Davis on Pushing Boundaries and Telling Stories That Matter," 2019. https://bostonconservatory.berklee.edu.

Scriptwriter

10. Quoted in Dan Jolin, "*Everything Everywhere All at Once*: The Story Behind an Unlikely $100m Hit," Screen Daily, November 30, 2022. www.screendaily.com.

11. Quoted in Richard Walter, "Richard Walter's Greatest Hits or The Reader's Backflip," Writers Store, November 24, 2020. www.writersstore.com.
12. Christina Ham, "Do I Need an Agent?," Playwrights' Center. https://pwcenter.org.
13. Quoted in Steve Walker, "By Nurturing a 23-Year-Old Playwright, the Living Room Creates Promising 'Junk,'" KCUR 89.3, December 10, 2015. www.kcur.org.
14. Scott Myers, "The Business of Screenwriting, 24/7/365," Medium, March 10, 2022. https://scottdistillery.medium.com.

Director

15. Quoted in Margy Rochlin, "Keeping His Cool," *DGA Quarterly*, Winter 2010. www.dga.org.
16. Quoted in Terry Gross, "*Wicked* Director Jon M. Chu Says Creativity Isn't Magic—It's Hard Work," *Fresh Air*, NPR, July 24, 2024. www.npr.org.
17. Quoted in Casey Mink, "How to Become a Theater Director," *Backstage*, April 12, 2021. www.backstage.com.
18. Quoted in Garth Franklin, "Directors Talk the Future of Theatrical," Dark Horizons, November 2, 2014. www.darkhorizons.com.

Production Designer

19. Quoted in Sam Cochran, "How the Set Design of the New Movie *Wicked* Ventures off the Beaten Yellow-Brick Road," *Architectural Digest*, September 17, 2024. www.architecturaldigest.com.
20. Quoted in Jaden Thompson, "*Wonka* Production Designer on Building a Whimsical City Based on Nostalgia: 'You Can Connect with an Audience That Way,'" *Variety*, December 16, 2023. https://variety.com.
21. Quoted in *Backstage*, "How to Become a Production Designer for Film, TV, and Theater," October 5, 2022. www.backstage.com.

22. Quoted in Lisa Granshaw, "*Knives Out* Production Designer Shares His Career Advice," *Backstage*, June 4, 2021. www.backstage.com.

Hair and Makeup Artist

23. Quoted in Film Connection, "Film Connection Graduate David Presto Wins Emmy," December 9, 2019. www.filmconnection.com.
24. Quoted in Cassie Carpenter, "The Magic in the Makeup," *Backstage*, November 5, 2019. www.backstage.com.
25. Annie Little, "How to Become a Hair and Makeup Junior: Annie's Story," BBC, 2025. www.bbc.co.uk.
26. Quoted in Marilyn Amato and Salma Loum, "Explaining Hollywood: How to Get a Job as a Makeup Artist," *Los Angeles Times*, June 8, 2022. www.latimes.com.
27. Quoted in Kirbie Johnson, "How CGI Changed Special Effects Makeup," *Allure*, November 20, 2021. www.allure.com.

Visual Effects Artist

28. Quoted in Joe Fordham, "John Dykstra, ASC: Finding Joy in the Process," *American Cinematographer*, July 13, 2023. https://theasc.com.
29. Quoted in Abby Stassen, "Computer Animation Grad Leads Award-Worthy VFX Teams," Full Sail Stories, February 23, 2022. www.fullsail.edu.
30. Quoted in Carlo Wolff, "Toward a Common Future: Disney and CIA Build on a Shared Past," Cleveland Institute of Art, March 13, 2024. www.cia.edu.
31. Quoted in Stassen, "Computer Animation Grad Leads Award-Worthy VFX Teams."
32. Quoted in Chris McGowan, "Streaming and VFX: Cultivating the Ability to Adapt to Constant Change," VFXV, January 7, 2025. www.vfxvoice.com.

Interview with an Actor/Director

Ron OJ Parson is the resident artist at Court Theatre in Chicago. He has been working as a stage actor and director for more than fifty years. He answered questions about his career by email.

Q: Why did you become a theater director?
A: Well actually I didn't choose this career; it chose me. As a third grader I was in a play at school, and it has become part of my life ever since then. Although I thought sports would be my way out, theatre took over and made me realize it was a viable choice for my future—with persistence and perseverance and a drive to succeed at something I loved doing. I had a career in New York, but mostly as an actor. When I got to Chicago, I started a theater company with Alfred Wilson called the Onyx Theater, and I was the artistic director there.

Q: What type of education and training has helped you along the way?
A: Since I started so early, junior high school, high school, and college were all big parts of my journey. I received a scholarship to the Studio Arena Theatre School in my hometown Buffalo, New York at age 13, and all that came into play—pun intended. I also started directing then, too as a teenager. At college, at the University of Michigan, I had doubts about theatre. But sports wasn't happening or working the way I wanted, so I became a journalism major—sports journalism to be exact. Ultimately, though, the theatre program won me over. During my freshman year at U of M is when I changed from journalism. I was walking in the theatre, the old Frieze Building, and heard a rehearsal of a play that came to my school when I was in the 7th grade. I recognized it as

Day of Absence, by Douglas Turner Ward of the Negro Ensemble Company. It changed my life and made me realize what I was supposed to be doing—acting. I got a part in it and my first acting teacher Robert McKee, who is now a famous author on screen-writing, also convinced me this was my path.

Q: Can you describe a typical workday?

A: I am an actor and director, so basically auditions and interviews are normal days. I also spend a lot of time reading plays, pitching plays, and, in preparing a play, rehearsing. Because of my body of work in my life and career I was able to be a resident artist at Court Theatre. That means I can direct, act, give my advice about the season planning, work with the community, develop new projects, or simply add my knowledge and expertise to the theatre. It's a rare position to be in for sure, but the main part of my career is as a freelance director and actor, which I was doing before Court Theatre, and I am sure to do after, too. I'm very proud to have been involved with 27 productions of August Wilson plays ("Fences," "The Piano Lesson," and others) all around the United States. Many people in the field get their MFA (Master of Fine Arts) and teach, but I never went that route. It is very different than a 9-to-5 job, that's for sure.

Q: What do you like most about your job?

A: Freedom. Being an artist is freeing in itself but very unpredictable. Of course I am in a unique situation as a residence artist. It's not your average actor/director situation, but the life of an artist is unique. That's what I like most.

Q: What do you like least about your job?

A: It's very hard to maintain consistent income in this industry. Again, my situation is different at this stage of my life. I am established, but usually you need a second form of income until you break through. And of course sometimes there is no breakthrough, but you continue because you need to, not just because you want to. It's an unpredictable life.

Q: What personal qualities do you find most valuable for this type of work?

A: Some of the most important qualities include perseverance, drive, creativity, persistence, love, heart, and openness to accept change. There are many situations where you have to adapt, so you have to be ready for that and be willing to adjust what you're doing and how you're doing it.

Q: What advice do you have for students who might be interested in this career?

A: Understand going in that it's hard work, but not impossible. Trust in yourself and be ready to work hard.

Other Jobs in Film, TV, and Theater

Acting coach
Agent
Animator
Assistant director
Casting director
Choreographer
Composer
Costume designer
Critic
Director of photography
Drama teacher
Editor
Focus puller
Grip
Lighting designer
Location manager
Lyricist
Music editor
Producer
Prop master
Publicist
Script editor
Set decorator
Show runner
Sound editor
Stage crew
Stage manager
Studio executive
Theater manager
Voice-over artist

Editor's note: The online *Occupational Outlook Handbook* of the US Department of Labor's Bureau of Labor Statistics is an excellent source of information on jobs in hundreds of career fields, including many of those listed here. The *Occupational Outlook Handbook* may be accessed online at www.bls.gov/ooh.

Index

Picture Credits

Cover: Dragon Images/Shutterstock

10: Alamy Stock Photo
26: Gorodenkoff/Shutterstock
35: Gorodenkoff/Shutterstock
43: CREATISTA/Shutterstock

About the Author

After graduating from the University of Oregon, James Roland became a newspaper reporter, primarily focused on education. He later became a magazine writer and editor, as well as an author of more than a dozen books. He and his wife, Heidi, have three children, Chris, Alexa, and Carson.